HORSE FARM

ARABIAN HORSES

ANNE ACCARDI

NORWOODHOUSE PRESS

Cataloging-in-Publication Data

Names: Accardi, Anne.
Title: Arabian horses / Anne Accardi.
Description: Buffalo, NY : Norwood House Press, 2027. | Series: Horse farm | Includes glossary and index.
Identifiers: ISBN 9781978580831 (pbk.) | ISBN 9781978580848 (library bound) | ISBN 9781978580855 (ebook)
Subjects: LCSH: Arabian horse--Juvenile literature.
Classification: LCC SF293.A8 A33 2027 | DDC 636.112--dc23

Published in 2027 by
Norwood House Press
2544 Clinton Street
Buffalo, NY 14224

Designer: Rhea Magaro
Editor: Kim Thompson

Photo credits: Cover, p. 1 Shchipkova Elena/Shutterstock.com; p. 5 Anaite/Shutterstock.com; p. 6 Kwadrat/Shutterstock.com; p. 7 U.S. Army; p. 8 AzizAlbagshi/Shutterstock.com; p. 9 Sari ONeal/Shutterstock.com; p. 10 S.O.E/Shutterstock.com; p. 11 Olga_i/Shutterstock.com; p. 13 pirita/Shutterstock.com; p. 14 fornaxstock/Shutterstock.com; p. 15 OlesyaNickolaeva/Shutterstock.com; p. 17 Dziurek/Shutterstock.com; pp. 18, 19 Alexia Khruscheva/Shutterstock.com; p. 20 Daniel Requena Lambert/Shutterstock.com; p. 21 Kaathi/Shutterstock.com;

Printed in the United States of America

CPSIA compliance information: Batch #CSNHP27: For further information contact Norwood House Press at 1-800-237-9932.

TABLE OF CONTENTS

Meet the Arabian Horse

The Arabian is a popular horse **breed**. Arabians have beauty and **spirit**. They hold their tails high. Their necks are long and **graceful**.

Arabians are from Asia. They were first bred in deserts thousands of years ago.

These horses form strong **bonds** with people. George Washington had an Arabian named Magnolia!

What Do Arabians Look Like?

Arabians are smaller than other riding horses.

They have strong legs. Their **hooves** are tough.

Arabian horses have wide foreheads.

They have big eyes.

Their **coats** can be many colors. Most are red, brown, or gray.

How Do Arabians Help People?

Arabians are smart. They are easy to train. They like to be around people!

Arabians have a smooth **trot**. They are great for riding.

They can run easily over different kinds of ground.

Arabian horses have great **endurance**. They can run hundreds of miles in one day.

They are also fast. They win many races.

What Do Arabians Need?

Arabians need healthy food. They eat grass, **hay**, and grains.

If they run a lot, they also need **protein**.

An Arabian should be cleaned every day. This keeps its coat smooth and shiny.

These horses do not like cold. In the winter, they need blankets and shelter.

Glossary

bonds (bahnds): close connections; strong feelings of friendship

breed (breed): one type or kind of an animal

coats (kohts): hair or fur that covers animals' bodies

endurance (en-DOOR-uhns): being able to do something hard for a long time

graceful (GRASE-fuhl): smooth and flowing

hay (hay): long grass that is cut, dried, and used as food for farm animals

hooves (hoovz): hard parts that cover the feet of horses, pigs, and other animals

protein (PROH-teen): a nutrient found in meat, nuts, and eggs that the body needs to build strong muscles

spirit (SPIR-it): courage and enthusiasm

trot (traht): movement that is faster than a walk but slower than a run

Thinking Questions

1. Where do Arabians come from?
2. What colors can Arabian horses be?
3. Describe an Arabian's head.
4. Why are Arabians good for riding?
5. What do Arabian horses need in the winter?

Index

About the Author

Anne Accardi is a librarian who loves reading books and learning new things! She lives in Kansas City, Missouri. When she's not writing, Anne enjoys listening to music, exploring nature around the city, and spending time with her family.